Stepping Stones to Success

Lydia M. Douglas

Published by Prioritybooks Publications
Missouri

Prioritybooks Publications
P.O. Box 2535
Florissant, Mo 63033

Copyright ©2005 by Lydia M. Douglas
All Rights reserved. No part of this book may be reproduced in any form without the consent of the Publisher, except brief quotes used in reviews.

Manufactured in the United States of America

Library of Congress Control Number: 2005905062

ISBN 09753634-2-5
Photograph by Ernest C. Sharpe
Cover designed by Chris House@Inkosidesigns
Edited by Jill Ronsley www.suneditwrite.com

For information regarding discounts for bulk purchases, please contact Prioritybooks Publications at 1-314-741-6789 or rosbeav03@yahoo.com, or Lydia M. Douglas at ldoug48305@aol.com.

Table of Contents

Stone 1- Fear is not an Option...... p. 1
Stone 2- Focus.......................... p. 5
Stone 3- Challenges.................... p. 9
Stone 4- Empowerment................ ..p. 13
Stone 5- Resolutions or Goals......... p. 20
Stone 6- Releasing your power...... p. 25
Stone 7- Satisfying the heart and soul..p. 30
Stone 8- Darkness of Racism............p. 34
Stone 9- Influence by Association......p. 38
Stone 10- Boomerang Theory..............p. 42
Stone 11- The Power of Persistence..... p. 46
Stone 12- Commitment....................p. 50
Stone 13- How do you measure...........p. 55
Stone 14- Becoming a goal achiever......p. 60
Stone 15- Values and Principles...........p. 65
Stone 16- How do you view your life?....p. 70
Stone 17- Positive Attitude..................p. 75
Stone 18- Finding the right path in life....p. 80
Stone 19- Diversity..........................p. 85
Stone 20- Change-the power of choice.... p. 89
Stone 21- Lessons Learned..................p. 93
Stone 22- Pain Relievers....................p. 97
Stone 23- Bridging the Gap.................p. 100
Stone 24- Defining your self worth.........p. 102
Stone 25- Fulfilling your dreams............p. 104
Stone 26- Success.......................... p. 106
Stone 27- Greatness versus Adventure......p. 110
Stone 28- This is my season.................p. 114
Stone 29- Mission Statement?...............p. 118

Acknowledgments

The idea to reach out to our young people started a decade ago. With so many interruptions, I kept starting and stopping. Since my retirement, I have had the opportunity to devote more time to what I truly believe in. I would like to give thanks to so many people who encouraged me to go ahead with this.

My first and foremost recognition must be given to my husband, James, for all his support and encouragement. He took my articles to work and passed them out, and he came home with great reviews. To my sons and their wives, Gerry and Angela, Mark and Michelle, and James Jr. and Stacye, thank you. They have been very helpful and supportive of me in this task. Whenever I have done presentations for local schools, they have been helpful and encouraging. They are patient when I call with a computer question. Thus, they have helped me to fulfill my dream. My mother, Mrs. Willie V. Savage-Coleman and stepfather Mr. Nathan Coleman, enjoys reading articles in the Spanish Lake Word News Paper as far away as Marianna, Arkansas. I would like to thank my pastor, Rev. Dr. F. James Clark. His review touched my heart in a way that he does not even know. Thank you, Pastor Clark.

A special thanks to Charlotte Petty, the editor of the Spanish Lake Word newspaper, for giving me an opportunity to serve as a guest columnist; and to my publisher, Rose Jackson-Beavers, who has shown her support from the beginning. Thanks to Victoria Whitfield, whose confidence in me allowed me to share my gift. Many thanks to Ishmael Sistrunk and Diane Page for your initial edit.

To my neighbors who have given me such great reviews, my heart was made glad by your insight. They all listened intently. Mrs. Delia Nordè, Linda Harris, Ruby Ellis, Sue Spaziano, and Yolanda Sims, who made sure she read my articles. To my sister-in-law, Sharon Savage, for her encouragement, and to my niece, Gwen Harvey, my cousin, Lee Anna Ellis and my sister, Alberta Hardy, who is waiting for the book signing. To the students in my life, it is for you that I write; for Jasmane Boyd, a student who responded positively to my work. I am thankful for the encouraging conversation I had with a young law student, Sharita Smith. I will continue to seek new ways to reach out to the students.

I would like to thank everyone who will support this book and pass the information along that is contained on its pages.

Shalom. Peace.

Dedication

This book is dedicated to my husband James H. Douglas for all your love, support and encouragement. To my sons, Gerry, Mark and James Jr., it is you who provided the inspiration and motivation for me to write this book to inspire other young people in their journey through life.

Foreword

What does it take to succeed? What is success? Is there a magic formula? These are questions everyone wants answered.

In Lydia Douglas' ***Stepping Stones to Success*** she helps youth or anyone concerned with the issues of life make good choices and find their own road to success. Lydia helps us see that success is what each of us discovers for ourselves using our God given talents and abilities. Praise God that success is not and should not be the same for us all which Lydia helps youth see as she takes them through facing challenges. All of our challenges are different which can bring us to different cross roads and fear. Lydia helps her readers confront fear and move on in spite of it.

An important tool Lydia uses in ***Stepping Stones to Success*** is the Boomerang Theory. Lydia makes it clear that what we give to life will come back to us and this should be important in guiding us, not just focusing on our own needs and desires. In the quest for success we must remember to reach out to others.

Stepping Stones to Success is a good guide in life if you want to read it from cover to cover, or refer to it when you need help on a specific topic such as dedication, fear, empowerment, or other topics. ***Stepping Stones to Success*** is a good boost in the important matters of life that can help or hinder success.

- *Charlotte Petty, Editor*
The Spanish Lake Word

Introduction

My Mission Statement

My mission and desire is that the heart of everyone who reads the words of this book may find something to identify with. Take it to the next level and allow it to encourage you to fulfill all your dreams. If the reader allows the words to impact his life, he will be able to share with others in order to impact theirs lives.

With all the negativity around us, it is important for me to focus on the good of others. If we share with others, we can learn from each other. There is a lot of good to be shared; we just need to re-focus. There is a proverb that says, "We teach what we need to learn most." My writing is about what I have learned and what I want others to learn. Each time I express it, I hear it again, too.

My purpose, values, and visions

To go deep within myself and decide what I want out of life; to make daily improvements to reach the next level; and to be proud of all my accomplishments, great or small. My purpose is to turn all negatives into positives. I realize that each day presents another lesson to be learned.

It's school time again. Because of this, my goal is to inspire the students to start thinking about what they want to do or become in their lives and to let them know that it is not too early to start making plans and preparations. I also want to get them to see that in order to "keep the dream and vision alive," first they must have one.

It's school time again. My purpose, values, and visions are these:

- To get the students to see that it's not only what's on the outside that counts, but it's what's on the inside, as well.

- To get them to ask themselves a powerful question: What are my goals, ambitions, and values in life?

- To raise the awareness that we have the power within us to become whatever or whomever we want to be.

Students just need to know how to tap into this well of untapped resources that all of us have within. I want the readers to leave with a new sense of mission, vision, and direction that can make a different in their lives. I write this book because of the children, because of the students and because I know that with guidance and direction, they can achieve all their dreams.

It's school time again. Let us all teach, train, and help the students attain their dreams.

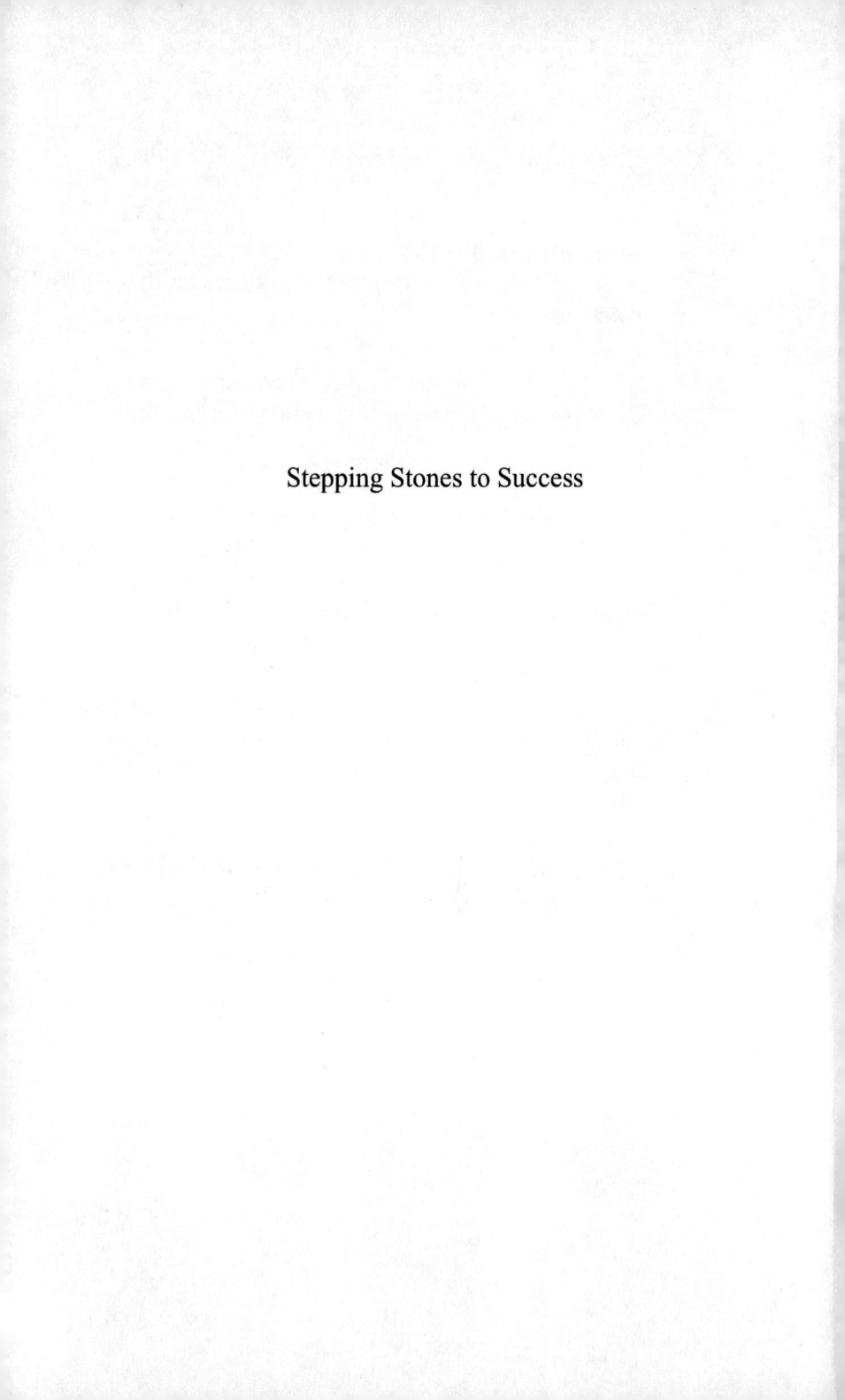

Stepping Stones to Success

Stepping Stones

Some stepping stones to dreams are small
Others are large and slick
Some have rough and ragged edges
For your weary feet to grip.

Some are spaced so far apart
Your legs will hardly reach
Others nest atop each other
Like pebbles on a beach.

For some you will need a leap of faith
On others, move with balance
A few will take uncommon grace
For most, your skill and talents.

You know the way, so just begin
Then keep a steady pace
Stretch and rest, and soon you will see
You have reached your special place.

Suzanne Zoglio

Stone 1:
Fear is not an Option
What do you fear?

Lydia M. Douglas

Fear is not an option

What is your biggest fear?

Failing your next exam? Being late for class or work? Graduating? Not getting accepted in the college of your choice? Failure has a strange secret. You become whatever you think about, because we are a combination of what we expose ourselves to and how we condition ourselves.

We live in a world of negative conditioning. But with our inner power, we can turn all negatives into positives. We have to get past the fear-factor, which sometimes will not go away.

Every day, we see and hear ads on TV that convey fear— fear of becoming sick from medicine the doctor prescribed, fear of food poisoning, fear of terrorism—the list goes on and on. But, with the assurance of the faith within you, you can and will make your visions come alive. Fear can intrude in the classroom, as well. When you take your seat, fear can pull up its own seat in your mind.

When this happens, if you allow it to be absorbed in your inner system, it will translate itself into failure. There are two key words here: "if" and "then."

In the midst of all the fear, we find ourselves struggling with success. Then we have to look failure in the face and tell it: "You might as well move on, because I am more than this."

I have struggled with many situations in life, but I made up my mind that I was not going to fail. I have always looked at failure from a different perspective. Failure is not an option for me.

If you exchange "I failed" with "I will learn from my choices," you will have a completely new mind-set. The option to fail is yours. We do have a choice, and our choices have consequences. We can either give into a negative thought or keep moving on. It's that simple.

Success or failure is up to us. We can fail to prepare. We can fail to be fully committed to whatever we are destined to do in life. We all have a destiny and purpose in life. Internal fears leads to external fears. Sometimes we allow our reactions to the internal to determine our destination. It's not so much what happened to you as what you do with what happens next. We all have choices. We can curse our choice, deny it, make excuses, blame others, or just quit.

Ask yourself the all-important questions: What have I learned? And what am I going to do about it? Failure only occurs when we decide to quit, and it is always too soon to quit. So, look for the why, and then find the solution. Perseverance and persistence will always work in your favor. Never allow your dreams to go unfulfilled. Sometimes, we might have to work a little harder than other people do. If that's what it takes, then just do it. After all, this is, your dream, and yours only. So, if the question is "How long do I try?" then the answer should be, "Until …"

The big challenge is to become all that you can be by stretching yourself to the limit. You will be surprised by what this will do for your inner being. All you have to do is decide what you want to do and what you are willing to give up or exchange for it, such as going to the movies, watching TV, or talking on the phone. Establish your priorities and don't relinquish them. Don't pay too big a price to pursue minor values. The difference between the impossible and the possible lies in a person's determination. Remember, the fear of failure is not an option.

Achievement requires more than a vision; it takes courage, resolve, and tenacity. When you look into the mirror, always see yourself the way you want to be. See yourself as strong, confident, and competent. The person you see is the person you will be.

Achievement equals the sum of ability and motivation. When you find the way to improvement, you have opened the door to strengthening your ability. After all, you are shaping your tomorrow with your thoughts and actions today. In your moment of decision, your destiny is shaped. One becomes successful the minute he or she decides to be.

Now, make the rest of the year become your year. You can do this once you realize that the most important option you have is the one that you hold. When the harvest time of your life comes, allow it to be good. We all reap just what we sow. If nothing is put in, nothing will come out. You cannot allow any circumstance from the past or present to abort future opportunities.

Stone 2:

Focus

Your short-term actions multiplied by time
equals your long-term accomplishments

FOCUS

You might ask yourself: "Focus? Why, when all I see are obstacles standing in my way?" Obstacles can't stop you, problems can't stop you, and other people can't stop you. Only you can stop you. And because of that ...

Now is the time to focus on your future. Your plans will miscarry if they have no aim. So, on that note you can begin to light your tomorrow with the brightness of today.

We are made wise not by the recollection of our past, but by taking the responsibility for our future. This school year is almost gone. My challenge to all students is this: Stay focused. The way in which each of us thinks will have a major impact on where each of us arrives.

Sometimes, change has to take place in our mind, judgment, and deeds. Our speech is an investment in the change that is about to take place. It is better to seek change through inspiration than out of desperation.

The tongue has the ability to speak negative and positive words. Our ears listen to what our tongue says. Change begins with our own power of choice. Life is change; growth is optional. We can choose to remain where we are or we can change—it's our choice.

If change is needed to reach your goals, visions and expectations, then you can use the 5-C Step Method. But you have to stay focused.

The 5-C Step Method:

1. Comprehend the importance of making changes.

2. Choose the change that's right for you.
3. Conquer all the fear that's holding you back.
4. Communicate your plans with others for support.
5. Commit to the changes that you have made.

We have the ability to change every aspect of our lives—starting today, forgetting yesterday, and looking toward tomorrow. Finals are not far off. If a plan of commitment is put in place now, by the time they come, you will be ready to soar to the top of the class. The closet of our mind holds old ideals and plans, but it also holds new ideals and goals.

Believe it or not, we all have the power to make our dreams come true. The advantage of being persistent is that all your surprises are good and pleasant. That's small change to what lies ahead.

Much of our happiness or unhappiness is caused by the results of our actions. The only misfortune comes when we suffer without learning the lesson behind our experience. By bringing change into our lives, we can chart our own destiny.

We reap what we sow. If we stay focused on our dreams, we decide what and how much we reap. There is no greater joy than knowing that you set your mind on something and accomplished it.

When ideals come to mind, stay focused, because you are producing seeds for great things right in the soil of your mind and heart.

Keep a sense of urgency, because without it desires and dreams lose their value. Action eradicates fear. No matter what you fear (if you fear anything), positive actions can diminish or completely cancel that which you are afraid of.

Ask yourself a question: "Who or what am I becoming?"—because today, you are writing your tomorrow.

Always remember, the worth of your life is not what you do or who you know, but by who you are. Why not be all you can be? You have talent, drive, and opportunities. Why not go for it? Become all you can and be all that you can. The best of your life is yet to come. The best is not set apart for someone else. Some of it belongs to you.

The key to the lock is that this is my time and I am going for it. Helen Keller said, "Never bend your head, always hold it high, look the world right in the eye." Helen Keller was blind and deaf. I hope this will help you to stay focused on your journey to greatness.

Write down the goals that you have for yourself, and then begin to prioritize them. Remember, these are your goals, born of your heart and mind. These goals will help you become the person that you were created to become. Your short-term action multiplied by time equals your long-term accomplishments.

Stone 3:

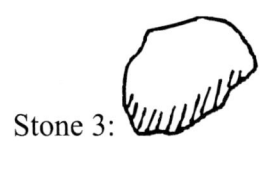

Challenges
What are your challenges that you face each day?

Challenges

We are faced with daily challenges, such as: What am I going to wear today? What hairstyle will go with my outfit? Do I watch this movie or do my homework? These are minor decisions that we have to make in life. And these have a quick fix. More serious ones face us, as well. Life's challenges can sometimes be overwhelming.

If you can look upon your challenges in a positive way, then you will be able to figure a way to approach them and learn from all of the issues that you will face along the way. Learning from past situations enables us to learn how to make changes in our lives. This should be the only time that you look back on life—for this reason and this reason only.

Believe it or not, there is a creative spirit within us, desiring to be free, and we might as well move over and allow it to come forth. We all are destined to be creative in some area or the other.

This creative spirit is like a giant that is asleep inside of you, and as soon as it is awakened, miracles begin to happen in your life. It is a personal challenge to be all that you can be, because a mind is a terrible thing to waste. Challenge yourself to greatness. Greatness is not just set aside for others. Look up, reach out, and get your share.

See yourself as a doctor, lawyer, engineer, teacher, or whatever you desire to be. Tell yourself you can become whomever or whatever you hope to be. I would like to encourage you to sit down and write a list of the expectations and desires you have for yourself. Then you will be able to see where you are now and what you need to

do to head in the direction that will lead you where you want to be. That can be a challenge in itself.
Then you will be able to ask yourself some valuable questions, such as:

1. Is this the direction I want for my life?
2. Is this someone else's direction?
3. Is this a goal that I have been entrusted to fulfill?
4. Is this my goal, my parents' goal, or someone else's goal?

After you have answered these questions, go a step farther, and ask yourself, "Am I headed in the right direction to become the person I want to be?" This process will take you one step closer to fulfilling your goals and creating the life you want to live.

A quote by Dr. Martin Luther King, Jr. states, "the ultimate measure of a person is not where he or she stands in moments of comfort and convenience, but where he stands at times of challenge and controversy." No matter what you come up against, never loose your desires. Your desires will be a stimulant to keep you motivated to fulfill your dreams.

We all have a destiny. And we are accountable to ourselves for creating that destiny. The true happiness of life has to start with you. When you set goals for yourself, you are half way there. All you have to do is figure out how to get from point A to point B.

There is a bridge between where you are now and where you want to be. You have to figure out how to bridge that gap. My son figured out how to bridge the gap in his life. He wanted to study computers so he went to South County

Tech to study. He became the sustainment manager for the number two cell phone company today.

Sometimes we have to face challenges head on. One main reason is that our choices have consequences and they affect us first. We reap what we sow, so why not sow some hard work and commitment into ourselves. Then, when the reaping begins, it will be great.

If you make a commitment, follow through on it. Remember, we are made wise not by the recollection of our past, but by the responsibility for our future. We are lighting our tomorrow by our action today.

The last thing to consider is this:

Creating your character is like an artist creating a sculpture. Character is the result of many choices you make that gradually turn who you are into who you want to be. Character is built by how you respond to what happens in your life. Now is the time to start chipping away at some of the things that may hold you back, and to keep chipping until you reach your goals. Remember, your short-term actions multiplied by time equals your long-term accomplishments.

Stone 4:
Empowerment
I have the power I need to move forward

Empowerment:

What do we mean by empowerment? Empowerment means you have the freedom to act. It also means you are in control of your life. And guess what! You are accountable for the results. And since you are accountable, the choices that you make have consequences, sometimes good, sometimes bad.

Each of you has two distinct choices to make:

1) You can choose to be less than what you have the capability to be; to earn less, have less, read less, or think less. These choices will only lead to an unfulfilled life.

2) You can choose to do it all and to become all that you can possibly be. To read more, earn more, share life more, and strive to produce and accomplish as much as you possibly can.

It all boils down to this: To be or not to be whomever or whatever you wish. Your life, my life, the life of each one of us is going to serve as either a warning or an example—a warning of the consequences of neglect or lack of direction and ambition, or an example of talents put to use, of objectives clearly perceived and intensely pursued.

When you make decisions that will affect your life, you need to keep three people in mind: me, myself, and I. Because whatever decision you make is going to affect you first.

Empowerment is not giving "power to the people." No one can give you power. It has to start with you. Rather, it is showing and encouraging you to release the knowledge, desire, potentials, experience, pride, and sense of self-motivation that you already have within.

There lies within each person a huge reservoir of untapped potential for achievement, success, happiness, health, and greater prosperity. It's like a huge ocean unsailed, a new continent unexplored, a world of possibilities waiting to be released and channeled toward some great good.

Remember the future belongs to you. So if you resolve in advance to persist until you succeed, then you will be successful at whatever you want to do in life. And while talking about other great people, why not become one yourself? Results are the best measure of human progress—not conversation, explanation, or justification. Results!

The miracle of the seed and the soil is not available by affirmation; it is only available by labor. The greatest rewards are reserved for those who bring great value to themselves and to the world around them as a result of who and what they have become. We have the ability to change our lives and our circumstances. We only need to know how to tap in this source of power within.

So how do you tap in this power?

1) You look deep within yourself and decide what it is that you want in life. What you want to be? Where you want to be?

2) You have to decide what direction you need to take. How you are going to get there?

Lydia M. Douglas

It is possible to fulfill your dreams. Empowerment isn't magic. It consists of a taking a few simple steps along the way with the recognition that there will be some bumps, and maybe some setbacks, but that with persistence and perseverance, changes can take place. Along life's journey, growth and maturity will take place if you allow them to. You should strive to be better today than you were yesterday.

My life has had quite a few ups and downs, setbacks, bumps—you name it and I've had it in my life. But I did not allow anything to stop me. Each pitfall just made me want to go further, sometimes in another direction. You can reach so much further in life if you don't have to start and stop many times along the way.

The choices and the paths you take in life are up to you. You cannot blame anyone else. Even at this late stage in life, I went back to school. I had a 4.0 grade point average, and I taught myself how to use the computer. (I asked my kids a lot of questions!)

Some of the choices I made in life landed me in places and positions that I would change if I were given the opportunity. But sometimes, when life hands you lemons—make lemonade! And keep adding a little sweetener along the way. A result of looking within is that new direction came forth.

All you have to do is make up in your mind as to what you want out of life and how to get there—and go for it. Empowerment allows you to take control of your life. You will never be able to act on this power if you are not sure of what you want out of life.

This is a good time to start thinking about your future. You can make your visions and dreams come alive when you see what you want for yourself and what direction you are going to take.

The way to create a compelling vision is to articulate a picture of yourself, an image that emotionally and intellectually clarifies the purpose of your being, your values, and your beliefs. This will illuminate your self-worth.

We all have a purpose in life. We just need to find out what it is. Be inspired to learn as much as you can, to gain as many skills as you can, to find a cause that benefits humankind, and you will be sought after for your quality of service and dedication to excellence.

Not everyone can be a teacher, lawyer, doctor, nurse, or other professional. We all have a purpose. Remember, always allow who you are on the inside to be who you are on the outside.

Let me share with you a conversation I had with a waitress at Steak n Shake. I asked her what school she went to and she told me she was waiting for her admissions papers to come back from University of Missouri in St. Louis. I asked her what she was going to study. She told me that she wanted to do research, because she has cancer. She went on to say that cancer runs rampant in her family, and due to the amount of sick days she has had, she did not graduate. She took the GED test and was able to get into UMSL. And because of her illness, she has decided to help find a cure for cancer.

Remember, you were created to innovate and accomplish, not merely to duplicate. This young lady will help find a cure for cancer—she won't just duplicate what's already out there. With the technology that is available and that which is to come, I am sure she will make a great contribution to research and the development of a cancer treatment and cure.

So many uncharted avenues exist today. Fresh minds and a new perspective are a welcome sight. Each person could have a different viewpoint but arrive at the same point.

So, I ask you all: Do not allow your dreams and visions to dissipate or slip away. You all are impregnated with so much knowledge, and you have resources available.

The ongoing challenges of your life do not abate or diminish, even while you are on the journey to your life's destination. So, you must stay focused in order to reach your goal.

While staying focused, you need to know all the facets of the career you plan. Research it with passion; that way, the best of you will truly come forth. Once this is done, no one will be able to take the wind out of your sail. Your dreams and visions will be the wind beneath your wings. Then, you will be able to soar to higher heights and deeper depths.

The stretch marks of life can be overwhelming at times. But if you prepare for life with all your heart and passion, you will be able to overcome them all. Birthing new ideas, new dreams, new visions, and new realities is possible only when you prepare yourself for the challenges of life. And that comes with hard work and determination.

Remember, you were created to innovate and accomplish, not merely to duplicate. And since you are impregnated with so much knowledge, you can be whatever you want to be; for example, you can research why babies are born abnormal and how older people can live longer. You can find cures for diseases. You have the knowledge and power to tap into all that exists. You can come up with new ideas and ways to make this world a better place.

It is possible to see yourself crossing the finish line of your goals and dreams, but first you have to believe that you can. Remember, you cannot allow anything or any circumstances to abort your future opportunities.

Through it all, I have learned that your choices do have consequences. I will leave with you valuable questions:

Will your choices make you happy or sad? What choices will you make?

Let others lead small lives, but not you.
Let others argue over small things, but not you.
Let others cry over small things, but not you.
Let others leave their future in someone else's hand, but not you.

The big challenge is to become all that you can be. I have found that there is no better time than now to get started on your dreams. You need to get an action plan and set your sights on the mountaintop. Remember, you cannot be successful if you have no vision or if you don't feel worthy of success.

Stone 5:
Resolutions or Goals
Have faith and courage in yourself

Resolutions or goals

Resolutions are what we say. Goals are what we achieve. I challenge you to get a plan and commit to it. The will to succeed is important, but what's more important is the will to prepare. No matter how busy you are, never fail to make a plan and work it.

Believe it or not, there is a creative spirit in all of us just waiting to be free. Goals get you going and allow you to live up to your greatness. Stevie Wonder says, "We all have ability. The difference is if and how we use it." This should ring true in your hearts. Know that you have the ability and life to make it happen.

Your association and influence plays a big part in goal-setting. We are all affected by everything around us, including what we read, what we watch, whom we talk with, and whom we spend time with. It all plays a part in how we view our world, our relationships, our opportunities, and most of all, ourselves.

The question is this: Resolutions or goals?

First, we need a plan. Our results are only as good as our plans. So you need to start the process of change by developing a plan. When you look at successful people, you can bet there was a plan behind their success.

Being successful is knowing what you want and working your plan in order to reach where you want to be. A good plan is the foundation for success. We as humans have a unique ability to make changes at any time in our lives.

How should you develop the right plan in order to reach the finishing line of your dreams in style?

1. Develop the right plan that includes your strengths and weaknesses.
2. Establish a time frame and stick to it as well as you can.
3. Keep a journal. Take notes on the ideals that impact you the most. Record your dreams and ambitions. When you write them down, they just seem more real.
4. Set Goals. Your plan is your roadmap for how you will reach where you want to be.
5. Act on your plans. If you don't, the excitement will dissipate.

If you don't act upon your plan, it will only be a dream, and a dream is just a dream. A goal is a dream with a plan and a deadline. It lets you know what you can do when your goals inspire you. There is no telling what you can do when you act upon your goals.

You have to define your goals, learn about them, and seriously consider them to be believable and achievable. Once you define and believe in yourself and the accomplishments that can take place, the victory is half won.

You might need to focus on one or two areas, but what's important is to focus. This could be a wake-up call for you in many areas of your life. Just tell yourself that this change is for me and me alone. Then your decisions will take on a different meaning.

The different between success and failure is not having a plan. And when you make your plan meaningful, it will come to pass. Goal-setting will add dimension, excitement, and texture to your life. Remember that your short-term actions multiplied by time equals your long-term accomplishments.

Here are a few tips that will create great accomplishments:
1. beliefs
2. visions
3. dreams
4. ideals
5. values
6. desires

These things will create and build your character and value system, and will create in you a high level of self-esteem. A huge well of untapped resources is sitting inside you, waiting for the opportunity to come forth. Once you do this, you will start to build an unshakeable character within yourself.

Then, obstacles cannot stop you, other people cannot stop you, problems cannot stop you. Only you can stop you. Once you get started, your goals and dreams will only grow with time. Always know that knowledge is power.

If a man empties his purse of the knowledge in his head, no one will be able to take it away. The seeds for great things are right there in the soil of your mind and heart. Once you attain this knowledge, it is your right to go forth and bring those dreams to life. Have faith and courage in yourself, and you will be able do whatever you want to do.

Courage is to dream anything you want to dream—that's the beauty of the human mind. To do anything you want to do—that's the strength of the human will. To trust yourself, to test your limits—that is the courage to succeed. Just say to yourself:

If my mind can conceive it,
And my heart can believe it,
Then I know I can achieve it. (Shalin Kirpalani)

Stone 6:
Releasing your power through reading
A mind is a terrible thing to waste

Releasing your power through reading

Knowledge is power, and it can be gained through reading. Once this power has been gained, you will be able to tap into the well of resources that you have within.

You will be able to open many doors for yourself just by reading books, novels, magazines, newspapers, and so on.

Reading will allow you tap into the great minds of others. Through reading, you will be able to expand your level of knowledge, and new ventures will open to you. It will also allow you to make better choices in life. Reading will help you draw the power that you are empowered with to make all your dreams come true.

It is truly amazing to see the human mind at work, for its capabilities are indeed endless. Yet it is very disheartening to see a mind go unchallenged.

Surely, a mind is a terrible thing to waste. Read and listen to positive materials. Fill your mind with positive and affirming words, ideas, and stories. Read materials that will enhance your skills or knowledge.

You may ask what type and how many books you should read. Well, it all starts with one and can go up to as many as will fit into your schedule. Reading biographies of successful people, you will find that many of them had problems in life but they overcame all of the negatives that were in their way. Now, you can say, "If they can do well, so can I." Reading and listening to positive material is about reinforcement, encouragement, and learning. All three of these components are needed for greater confidence.

Stepping Stones to Success

It can all start with you taking the time to read. Reading will allow you to stop going with the flow and start your own river instead. You do not have to follow the crowd.

You do not have to conform to your surroundings; you can be transformed by the renewing of your mind through reading. By taking this approach, you will know whether what you are doing is good and right for you. This will also allow you to measure your worth.

I know a very bright and smart young lady whose name is Markia. She reads on average of ten to fifteen books per week. She goes to the library every Tuesday and checks out the books she wants to read, and by the following Tuesday, she has finished reading all of them. Her parents thought she was cheating until she gave them a review of the books she had read. By the way, Markia is thirteen years old and maintains an A average in school.

Now, this may be a high number for everyone to read each week, but remember, it all started with one book. Markia lives in San Antonio, Texas with her parents and brother. Hopefully, one day she will be able to go to some of the local schools and share her reading experiences with others: how and when she became interested in reading and what and how much she has accomplished through her reading. When someone else sees the joy you have in reading, they will be encouraged and will feel they can do the same. Reading will raise you self-esteem to the next level. When you read about the accomplishments of others, then you can tell yourself again:

If my mind can conceive it,
And my heart can believe,
Then I know I can achieve it. (Shalin Kirpalani)

Remember again: "Defeat is optional, and I am not going to take that option." Small accomplishments can be stepping stones to larger ones as you begin to discover what you really can do.

Since our attitude is greatly shaped by influence and association, if you hang around thinkers, you will become a better thinker; around a planner, you will become a better planner; and around readers, you will become a better reader.

Another thing that will shape your attitude: Don't join an easy crowd in which you will not grow. Go where you can take your expectations to the next level and where the demands are high. Why not become all you can be, every moment you can? Why not be the best you can for as long as you can?

You must constantly ask yourself these questions:

- Who am I around?
- What are they doing to me?
- What have they got me reading?
- What have they got me saying?
- Where do they have me going?
- What do they have me thinking?
- And most important, what do they have me becoming?
- Then ask yourself the big question: Is this what I want for me?

Books will allow you to accelerate your abilities or you to attempt to achieve higher levels of what you are already good at. Never allow your memory to be greater than your dreams. Character maybe manifest in great moments, but it is made in the small ones. One big appearance does not make you. It is the smaller ones over time that really count and will last longer in the mind of others.

So why not start with a book?

Stone 7:
Satisfying the heart and soul
Your dreams and passion will not dissipate or go away

Satisfying the heart and soul

I can be changed by what happens to me,
But I refuse to be reduced by it.

This is one of my favorite quotes by poet Maya Angelou. When we are passionate about something, we have to look deep within our heart and soul and fulfill those dreams. If you are not happy with your life, then others around you will not be happy with you either. Every thing and everyone you touch will feel the affects. Once you are happy with your life and the direction you are headed in, you will see a much brighter future for yourself.

There are some dreams inside of you that have been longing to come out. Now is the time to bring your dreams to life. Do not spend your life wishing it were different. Even though you might not be where you want to be at this time, with hard work and persistence, you can be all that you want to be. Your dreams and passions do not dissipate or dissolve. You are empowered with the strength that you need to execute whatever it is that you are passionate about.

You need to remind yourself that the future belongs to you. So you have to resolve in advance to persist until you succeed. In order to succeed, you have to be relentless in your efforts. It usually does not happen overnight. Each of us has within himself a talent of some sort to achieve success, but the key is to have the ability to identify and develop your own particular talent or gift. Regardless of what you think, we all have something magical to share and express. There is an artist of some type in all of us, and each of us has two distinct choices to make:

First Choice:

You may choose to be less than what you can be, to earn less, to have less, to read less, or think less. Any of these choices will only lead to a life of unfulfillment.

Second Choice:

You have a choice to do it all, to become all you can possibly be, to read more, to earn more, to share life more—to strive to produce and accomplish as much as you possibly can.

It all boils down to this: To be or not to be whomever or whatever you want to be. You need to remind yourself that it is time to go forth with what you want to do in your life. Each day that pass is one day less that we have. You must spend your days wisely. They will pay off in the long run.

We all have a purpose in life. We just need to find out what that purpose is. Always allow who you are on the inside to be who you are on the outside. You cannot allow anything or any circumstances to abort future opportunities.

Always remember:

The worth of your life comes not from what you do or who you know, but from who you are. You yourself are very important. Spend some time with yourself and discover who you really are.

Finally, work hard, enjoy yourself, keep your spirits high, and don't ever give up. Say to yourself:

Once again:

Believe in yourself, and no mountain will be too high!

Stone 8:
Darkness of racism
Underneath we are all the same

Darkness of Racism

Racism. Animosity shown to people of a different race. A Rabbi was doing a lecture on "Race and Diversity." In the midst of his lecture, someone asked a powerful question: How can we tell when night has passed?

- Is it when we awake and it is daylight?
- Is it when we have rested after a long, hard day?
- Is it when we can tell a peach tree from an apple tree?
- Is it when we can go any place we care to go?

The answer is no to all the above. It is when we can look at the face of any man or woman, boy or girl, and see him or her as our brother or sister. If you cannot see this, it is still night, because underneath it all, we are all the same. Night is this:

- When we hear someone speak who we don't know and say that's not my language
- When we hear them pray and say that's not my religion
- When we see what they eat and say that's not what I eat
- When they dress and we say that's not my style
- When I see their skin and say it's not the color of mine

BUT

- When they laugh, it's how I laugh

- When they hurt, that's how I hurt
- When they need water, I need water
- When they need air, I need air
- When they cry, it's how I cry, and the tears flow the same

When we can see and accept this in our heart and soul, we will know that night has passed. It is now time to move from night into the sunlight of acceptance. You will prepare yourself for a unique journey to wholeness. We have to confirm our feelings, challenge our emotions, and change our views.

In retrospect, we can all look back and glean lessons from the past. And now, we can look at things with a different perspective in mind. In so doing, you will have a new transformation of what your heart feels and what your eyes see. We all came into this world wrapped in only skin, and it was a wonderful way for all of us to begin.

But what matters most from the day we began is the gift that we have, and the ability to share ourselves with others—and it all comes from within. We are all caught in an inescapable network of mutability or change. We are clothed in a single garment of destiny. Whatever affects one affects us all in some way or other.

As we recite the Pledge of Allegiance, let us focus on "I" and "all." The pledge begins with I and ends with all. I pledge allegiance … with liberty and justice for all. That's what we should be about: I as an individual and all as all of us. When we all understand how valuable each of us is, then each of us will understand how powerful we all are.

So many gifts have been deposited in America that we all have something to share with others. We can create a world where all the gifts can be displayed at ease.

I am convinced that the family a person grows up in or the color of someone's skin should by no means control his or her destiny.

Mother Teresa stated, "Kind words can be short and easy to speak, but their echoes are truly endless."

The same holds true with harsh words. There has been a wedge of division for much too long. Believe it or not, you are your brother's keeper. We as a people should value the inner person, not the outer person. We have no power over this outer person, but we do have control over the inner person.

Sometimes, it's better to look at the contents of a person and not the container. If we open our eyes, souls, and hearts, we can begin to celebrate our common humanity.

CRAYONS:

We can all learn a lot from crayons. Some are sharp, some are pretty, some are dull, some have weird names, and they are all different colors. But they all have learned to live in the same box. So let's become like a box of crayons!

Stone 9:

Influenced by association
Believe in yourself

Influenced by Association

There are two parts to influence:

   A. Influence is powerful
   B. Influence is subtle or very quiet and easy

You will not allow someone to push you off course, but someone can nudge you off course, one nudge at a time, and you will not even realize what's going on. You cannot get all the answers from one source or one person. A variety of sources is best. Our attitudes are so powerfully shaped by influence and association.

Don't spend a lot of time on voices that do not count. Tune out the shallow voices so you can have more time to tune in to the valuable ones. The people you hang with will be a great influence on your life. Believe it or not, you are shaping and molding your tomorrow by your attitude today.

It does not matter who you are or what side of town you live on. Gender is not a factor. It's what you have on the inside that matters. It's the size of your dreams, goals, and visions that matters.

Hang around people who have something of value to share with you. Their lives will impact yours long after you have parted company. Then, in your everyday life, you will have learned how to win friendship and influence people, for you will have an impact on their lives, as well.

My first piece of advice is this: Believe in yourself. If you have enough determination to achieve your goals, there is nothing that can stand in your way. Small accomplishments can be steppingstones to larger ones as you begin to discover what you can do.

You are empowered from within with everything you need to fulfill all your dreams. Now, figure out what you want out of life and find the path you need to take to reach there. That way, all your dreams can come true. Play your strengths and try to improve your weaknesses. Then, you will be on the way to finding your purpose in life.

We all have a purpose in life, but it's up to us to find out what that purpose is. By being involved with the right people, this will truly be an important and enjoyable time. You will discuss talents and dreams that you didn't realize you had. Try to strike a balance between what you want to do and what you need to do in order to bring your dreams to light.

Days are expensive. When you spend one day, you have one day less to spend. So make sure you spend each one wisely. Results are the best measurement of human progress. Not conversation. Not explanation. Not justification.

RESULTS

Work is an extension of personality. It is achievement. It is one of the ways a person defines himself and measures his self-worth and humanity. If our results are less than our potential suggests that they should be, we must strive to be more today than we were yesterday.

The greatest rewards are always reserved for those who bring great value to themselves and the world around them because of who and what they have become.

Finally, work hard, enjoy yourself, and don't ever give up.

Again, say to yourself:

If my mind can conceive it.
And my heart can believe it.
Then I know I can achieve it. (S. Kirpalani)

Success is waiting for you because defeat is optional!

Stone 10:
Boomerang Theory
What you throw out will come back to you

The Boomerang Theory

First, a boomerang is an angular club with a cut out. You toss it away from you, and it eventually returns. In the game of life, you throw the boomerang daily in the form of actions, reactions, behaviors, and attitude.

Each day, we are throwing out our self-worth, and each day, it will return to us one way or the other. Our self-worth is how we perceive ourselves.

We've all heard the old saying "What goes around comes around," and the scriptures that say, "What a man sow that he shall reap" or "Give and it shall be given unto you." The returns can be negative or positive. For example, if you are critical and judgmental all the time, don't be surprised when it returns unto you in the same manner. Always try and be fair and honest, this will be returned to you in some form or the other.

Now, there are some misconceptions about the Boomerang Theory. You have to view it from a long-term perspective. There could be a possible delay, but you will reap what you sow sooner or later. That's why we have to be accountable for our actions as well as our reactions. Since we are accountable, let's think hard and twice about what we say and do, because whatever we may do and say, we are indeed putting our self-worth on the line.

We need to ask ourselves: Are we happy with our attitude, our work, and our response to others? We should answer with more yeses than noes. We can begin to work on the no's today. Just remember, when you withhold good deeds from others—something as simple as a smile, a hello, or a good-bye—the same will be withheld from you. If we refuse to be kind and helpful to others, these same deeds will be withheld from us. Our actions toward others will activate the flow of the boomerang of kindness back to us.

The Bible also says, "Do unto others as you would have them do unto you." If you want people to be kind to you, you must be kind to others.

Allow me to share a testimony. I pulled onto the parking lot of one of our local grocery stores. I parked and then noticed that someone had left a large container of Tide Laundry detergent in the bottom of a cart. I took it, put it in my car, went into the store, and did my shopping. As I was putting my grocery into the car, I looked at the Tide bottle and felt bad. I went back into the store and asked a clerk what the store would do if someone brought an item back inside that had been forgotten by another customer. She told me, "If someone brings an item back and the customer who bought it calls to see if it had been turned it in, that customer can return to the store and get the item they purchased." This is what I did. I returned the item to the store. Now, when I did that I felt good within myself.

When I got home, there was a check in the mail that I did not know I was going to get. Some time earlier that week, I had received a rebate gift card in the mail. I don't even remember buying anything from that store, but I called and was told that the check was mine and I could use it. These are boomerangs returning themselves back to me.

Monitoring our actions will allow us to have positive visions for ourselves. All our good deeds are deposited in the Universal Bank of Life. They are earning compound interest, and we will receive the dividends in due time. When the boomerang is returned, it is just what we need at the time. I have learned that one should always do what one says he or she is going to do, because one's self-worth is on the line.

Our attitude shapes our destination. With this in mind, we can allow our imagination to sore to heights unknown, and our lives will always include others.

A little watch list for your thoughts:
1. Watch your thoughts, for they become your words.
2. Watch your words, for they become your actions.
3. Watch your actions, for they become your habits.
4. Watch your habits, for they become your character.
5. Watch your character, for it becomes your destiny.

What lies behind us, and what lies before us are small matters compared to what lies within us. If you can keep this in mind, it will be the wind beneath your wings. It will allow you to measure the true measure of your self-worth. When the boomerang returns, it will be on a positive note.

When we share ourselves with others, we can overcome the thorns that may be on our path. This will allow the rose in us and in others to blossom many times over.

The greatest good you can do for another person is not share your riches, but to reveal to him his own.

Stone 11:
The Power of Persistence
Only **you** have the power to stop you

The Power of Persistence

The word persistence, according to Webster, is a state or action in spite of obstacles or objections. Persistence is the power to hold on in spite of everything else. It allows you to endure and to conquer all obstacles that may get in your way. While talking with successful people, each one stated that persistence was the key. Looking back, had they not been persistent and had they given up, they would not have made it through the tough times.

Persistence equips you with the power to look at every stumbling block clearly and say, "I am more than this. If I have to go in another direction, I will." Continue moving on. There will be some pain, setbacks, and disappointments along the way, but if you are determined, this, too, shall pass.

I am a true believer in the fact that if you work hard for what you want and believe in what you are trying to do, you will be successful. While working hard at reaching your goals, once you get to the point where you want to be, it will be more valuable to you because you worked for it rather than having someone hand it to you.

My father told my siblings and me, "If you want something out of life, work for it, and when it's yours, no one will be able to take it from you." The same holds true for goals, dreams, and visions. They grew out of your heart and your inner being. No one and no circumstance will be able to take that away from you. The same holds true for education. Once you get it, no one will be able to take it away. If you empty your purse of knowledge into your head, it's yours forever. If you add discipline, persistence, and sacrifice, they will measure less than a meter against a lifetime. This is only possible if you are persistent. Because truly, a dream is only a dream until it is put into action.

There are prices to pay in order to reach our goals, such as not going to a movie, shopping, or out to eat. But that's a small price to pay when measured against a lifetime of happiness, contentment, and satisfaction with your choices in life. Sure, you are going to hit some rough spots now and then, but with a made-up mind, you can and will overcome them.

You might have to change directions, but that's the advantage of having the power of choice. There are many avenues to cross. Just decide which one is right for you and keep moving toward your goals. We all have the desire to do well. Sometimes we make mistakes along the way, but we forge ahead anyway.

A person should only look back to see where he or she went wrong and learn from it. When you know all the whys and hows of your mistakes, you will be able to put them in perspective. That way, you will not repeat the same error.

One other thing is to prioritize and ask yourself, "What is more important: enjoying life or preparing for a better one?" Write down your goals and review them daily. When you write them down, you will be able to see the whole picture at once.

That's why it is so important to be on the track that's right for you. You cannot fulfill someone else's dream and be happy. This time, it's all about you.

Mentally and intellectually, paint a picture in which you are doing what you want to do. Then your dream will become clearer to you. Once your goals are set, you will see the way more clearly to achieve them. Then, you will see that going to the library is more important than going to the party.

The importance of finding a career that you are happy with cannot be overstated. Allow your past to be your motivation for your future. A world of incredible opportunities awaits you. Focus your attention on the great adventures ahead. Have a mission statement for yourself.

This is my life:

I promise that I will take charge of the direction and quality of my life.
I alone am responsible for my actions.
I will not blame others for my failures.
I will work diligently and constantly to improve who I am and what I am.
I will be proud of every accomplishment, however small.
I will recognize that each step brings me closer to my goals.
Each failure is but a lesson to be learned.
I will be courageous and face my fears, knowing that in doing so, my strength will increase.
This is my life. I will live it to the fullest.

Stone 12:
Commitment
The first commitment should be to yourself

Commitment

We all have made commitments in life. The question is whether we have lived up to those commitments or they were just words going up in smoke. The fact that our choices do have consequences is both good and bad. I made some bad choices in my younger years and faced the consequence of doing a job for many years that I did not want to do. But I made the best of it and was always looking to the future for change. Even though it took a long time coming, it came. Through years of perseverance and struggle, I made it through. Today is a new day. Things are much different than they were then.

When you have a family, bills, and responsibilities, it is very hard to make up for the wrong choices that you made. It was very difficult to work hard during the day and go to school at night. In the middle of the semester, my working hours would change and all that time went down the drain. But I was committed to doing what I wanted to do, and that was to go back to school. I had a made up my mind that I was not going to settle for the low end of life. So I persevered each and every day.

My point is that your choices do have consequences. Are you ready for the consequences of your choices and actions? It is much better and easier to get to the point of your dreams before you are committed to family matters. Think things through long and hard before making decisions that will affect your life and the lives of the ones that are closest to you.

We all have a purpose in life. We just need to figure out what it is. Our purpose is the key to a fulfilled life. When you find or figure out your purpose, make a commitment to fulfill every aspect of that purpose. If you tell yourself you can do a certain thing, you will succeed. Success is not what you think it is. It is what you believe it is. All you need is the will and determination to succeed. A commitment could be to stop smoking, to stop unhealthy eating, to get more exercise, to stop drinking, or to change something as simple as watching too much television.

Ask yourself if what you are committed to will allow you to make your long-term commitment. If the answer is no, it is time to start over and go in another direction. All you need is the will and determination to succeed. Start by cleaning out the closet of your mind. Discard ideals that no longer fit your lifestyle or the expectations you have for yourself. Then, go deep within yourself and figure out what you want to do with your life.

Life is not easy for anyone, but it can be much easier when you have a commitment. Just believe you will succeed, no matter the cost. The only limitations we have are the ones we put on ourselves. All things are possible. You just have to believe they are.

You are always free to choose what you do with your life. The choices are yours to make. One thing to remember is to make changes or choices out of inspiration, rather than desperation.

Change comes from one or two sources.
1. We may be driven to change out of desperation. Sometimes, our circumstances can be so out of control that desperation drives us to look for a solution.
2. A drive from within to make changes in our lives can also come from inspiration. Hopefully, this is

where you find yourself right now. Be inspired to make the necessary changes in your life.

Whatever your dreams are they will not dissipate or go away. They will forever be in your heart. You can change the direction of your life any time you want to do so. It can start the moment you decide to make a change. Do not allow yourself to get pushed into a corner, for valuable time will be wasted. Time not well spent is time wasted.

Develop a clear vision for yourself. Talk to others who can give you positive feedback or advice. Listen to them. When you are cleaning out the closet of your mind, sometimes you might have to toss out old friends. If they cannot help you or encourage you, maybe it's time to move on.

Don't hang around voices that do not count. Look toward people whose lives will have an impact on you, and maybe your life can impact them as well. Always be eager to learn something new. Be a leader, not a follower. Don't just go with what someone says. Take an interest in it, and then debate it. See how it lines up with your beliefs. This will allow you to see how to take your dreams to the next level. Never allow yourself to think negatively about yourself.

Sometimes, all you need is a new set of lenses in order to view life from a different perspective. Yesterday's visions will not always fulfill tomorrow's goals. Your life, my life, and everyone's life is going to serve as either a warning to stay away from something or as an example.

Which do you prefer? Your life will have a harvest time. That's when you will be able to look back and see how you have profited and how your life has turned out. You want to be able to answer the question: Has my life been a mission or an intermission? You want your response to be positive.

At the end of each day, when you play back the tapes of your performances, the results should applaud, prod, or chastise you. Which do you prefer? The choice is yours.

When you choose to commit, remember that your commitment will be with you throughout your lifetime. It will help you always to keep your priorities in order. It will allow you to be independent in life, because you will be able to make better choices for yourself, to modify your dreams or magnify your skills.

In the process:
Don't wish it were easier; wish you were better.
Don't wish for fewer problems; wish for more skills.
Don't wish for fewer challenges; wish for more wisdom.
Remember, you are accountable for the choices you make.
Do not allow things or circumstance to abort your future opportunities.

Stone 13:
How do you measure your self-worth?
Self-worth—think about it!

How Do You Measure Your Self-Worth?

Self-worth is how one views oneself. How do you view yourself? Is it by the profits of your life or by the mistakes that have been made along the way? Is it by what others say about you, or is it the path you are on? Is it when you use scurrilous or abusive language?

Take a good view of your life before answering any of the questions above. Look inside yourself and figure out how you feel about life. After you have asked yourself these questions, debate them. After you have answered them, ask another question: What am I doing that is working or not working?

Your self-worth comes from the inside, not the outside. You should always allow the person inside to be the person who is outside. Whatever you are doing, whether on the job, when shopping, while communicating with others, or when just being you, always allow your best to come forth.

For example, if you go shopping, pick something up, and put it back, don't just put it back in any way. Your self-worth is more than that. Do unto others as you would have them do unto you. If you are at your job, do the best that you can, because it is a reflection of you. When you sign your name on any form or document, remember, you are putting yourself on the line.

How do you measure your self-worth? You do it by every good deed you have on the inside. Even if you have made some mistakes in judgment, it does not or should not alter who you are on the inside. You must have a sense of direction for your life. And that will make a measurable difference in how you view your self-worth.

Your self-worth is the character within you. You were not born with it—you have to create it on your own. You should care about how others perceive you. Even though you are not responsible for what people say and feel about you, reflecting on these things will allow you to ask yourself: How do I carry myself?

When you apply for employment, how will the potential employer perceive you? Even though he is looking on the outside, will he or she be able to see the inner you?

How do your neighbors, family, and friends perceive you? Sometimes, you might have to chisel away old attitudes in order for the one that is deep within to come forth.

If you really want to bring this character out, you will not only create great qualities, but you will continue to strengthen them, because this will be who you really are.

With each day, you will recreate them in abundance and multiply them with action or deed. You will use them, but you will never use them up. When your self-worth is formed, it will serve as a solid, lasting foundation upon which to build the life you want for yourself.

You contain within yourself a unique combination of talents and abilities which, when properly identified and applied, will enable you to achieve virtually any goal you set for yourself.

Once you know who you really are, work to expand your vocabulary. A good vocabulary enables you to express yourself so that you are perceived by others in the way that you want to be perceived.

Well chosen words mixed with emotions affect people. Words do two major things: provide food for the mind and create light for understanding and awareness. While working on your self-worth, resolve in advance to persist until you succeed, no matter what difficulty you might encounter along the way.

In doing so, you will bring your self-esteem to a much higher level. The more you like yourself, the less fear you have of anything. Overcoming fear happens by acting as though failure is impossible; then, the death of fear will be certain.

After you conquer fear and doubt about who you are, you will be able to see clearly that with today's actions, you are purchasing your tomorrows. There are no limitations to what you can be, have, or do, except the ones you place on yourself. Challenge in life is inevitable; defeated is optional. Do not make defeat your choice.

Just know that life is filled with many golden opportunities, even though sometimes they are diagnosed as impossibilities. If you put forth all your effort and do your best, nothing is impossible for you.

You have a tremendous reservoir of potential within, and therefore, you are quite capable of doing anything you put your mind to. Remember, the most important opinion about you is the one you hold. Ultimately, no one else is responsible for your life but you. No one else is accountable for your actions. Therefore, no one's opinion about you should be more important than yours.

Say to yourself again:
If my mind can conceive it
And my heart can believe it
Then I know I can achieve it
Your self-worth is all up to you.
Upon doing this, the illumination of your self-worth will be brought forth.

To help reinforce your greatness, I ask you to repeat this phrase often throughout this book.

Stone 14:

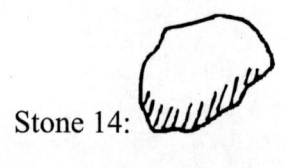

Becoming a Goal Achiever
Will your plans allow you to achieve your goals?

Becoming a Goal Achiever

If you know what you want to do in life, you are well on your way to achieving your goals.

Things to think about:
1. Select and prioritize your goals.
2. Bring your body, mind, and spirit together in order to realize your dreams.
3. Figure how or what you need to do in order to bridge the gap between where you are and where you want to be.
4. Use a sensible approach when deciding what you want out of life.

Select and prioritize your goals:
Decide what your goals are and where you want to be in life. No matter what your goals are, you are going to put them in place, because your choices will affect you and your life. Do not allow anyone else to set your goals for you. After all, you are the one that will pursue them.

Bring your body, mind, and spirit together:
No matter what it you want to do, tell yourself you can do it. If you don't try, how will you know that you can't? Once you bring your body, mind, and spirit together, you will be able to figure out what you need to do in order to get it done. Check your list and discard the goals that are no longer of interest to you.

Bridge the gap:
Figure out what you need to do in order to bridge the gap of where you are now and where you want to be. If that means going back to school, then by all means, go back. Maybe

you just want to take a special course. Then do it. You cannot become a doctor without going to medical school.

Use a sensible approach:
Be realistic in your thinking. Do not waste time on things that are not realistic for you.

Develop the attitude that attracts the support and assistance you need to reach your goals. Then, look at a time line to see if you can make it happen or not.
Begin to investigate, and then eradicate all the problems that could possibly hold you back from achieving your goals.

When this is done, take on the responsibility of doing what you need to do. Remember, there are no free rides. This will help you to internalize your vision. It will be with you daily, in everything you do. You will see yourself in it.

Be persistent about getting all the details and road maps that you need. There is so much information available that there is no excuse not to reach your goal.

By being persistent and making bold decisions, you will see internal growth take place. You will no longer be afraid to take risks. And the enemy of fear will no longer lurk inside of you, telling you that you will not succeed, but you will fail. Once your attitude has changed, you will be in complete control of your thoughts and your inner being.

Self-doubt will be then replaced with confidence. Having confidence in your ability to achieve will improve every aspect of your life. Always remember that a man's dreams are his index to greatness. In order to reach your level of greatness, you have to build your courage and be able to fight what's holding you back from reaching the level you want to reach. You have to be courageous in your life and in your pursuit of the things you want and the person you want to be.

In becoming a goal achiever, let's look at the 5-C's of life:
1. Character: your internal makeup. It's who and what you are about on the inside, which will flow to the outside.
2. Credibility: Are you credible? Is your word true? Your words and actions coincide with each other.
3. Capacity: Are you able to look to the future and perceive what might happen or what may be the outcome of what you are doing or want to do?
4. Courage: This is your inner strength. It will allow you to overcome anything might gets in your way.
5. Communication: the ability to translate your visions into actions.

In order to be a goal achiever, you must search, because ideals can be life-changing and help to shape your life. Life is filled with golden opportunities. Not all of them belong to other people; some of them belong to you.

While reading about great minds, why not become one yourself? Take possession of what belongs to you!

We are all in possession of the most powerful tool that we could have. That tool is our mind. The mind has the ability to think and bring into focus your life, disappointments, and resolutions.

The more reasons you have for achieving your goal, the more determined you will become. The results will come forth with all your hard work. You will be a winner at achieving your goals. Keep in mind that you are lighting your tomorrow by your actions today. If you do nothing today, today is wasted and you cannot get it back. Then tomorrow will be packed with what should have been done today.

Results are the best measure of human progress—not conversation, explanation, or justification. Results!

When you wake up in the morning, start the day with this statement:
My purpose is to do _____ today.

Each night before going to bed, complete the following statement:
I am thankful for _____ today.

Remember, the future belongs to you. If you resolve in advance to be persistent until you succeed, you will be successful at whatever you want in life.

Stone 15:

Values and Principles
Like a glove, they go hand in hand.

Values And Principles

The major value in life is not what you get. It is who you become. That's a good thing to keep in the forefront of our mind. Example: In life, if I have to pay for something or work for it, I will view the item or accomplishment with a sense of pride. If I get it for free, the value is less.

In matters of style, you can change at any time of the season, but in matters of principle, morals, and values, we should stand as solid as a rock. Your principles and moral values go hand and hand. If whatever you believe in your heart is right, of course, stay with that.

A question for you and all of us should be: How do I value myself? Sometimes we do things because we can, sometimes to please others, and sometimes, just because we are big enough and bad enough—and with that, we put our self-worth on the line. Always decide what's right before you decide what's possible. Life is an ongoing process of keeping your visions and values before you and aligning your life to be congruent with or equal to those things that are true in your heart. Success, happiness, and peace of mind are the prize for those who stand true to their ideas and values.

When you are true to your values, you will be able to conquer, overcome, or overpower whatever may come in your way, try to turn you aside, and cause you to lose your focus on your goals.

I have learned, and you can, too, that if you keep your eyes on your goals and the sunshine of life, you will not be able to see the shadows of darkness. And if and when you do come to a dark area, you will be able to fix, correct, or address the situation and keep moving on. If and when we encounter bad situations, we must look for the good.

The good could be seeing the mistakes that were made or the path you are on. We all make mistakes in life. We may be rejected, but no matter what, we must look at the errors that have been made as detours on the road to success.

Becoming unstoppable by refusing to quit, no matter what happens, is one of our human qualities. Remember, you are the only one who has control over your values. If you have enough determination to achieve your goals, nothing can stand in your way.

Even on your journey to becoming the successful person you want to be, small accomplishments can be stepping stones to larger ones, as you begin to discover what you really can and want to do. We cannot achieve the success we want by remaining the person we are.

Sometimes we have to accelerate our abilities:

For those who will achieve much are those who say to themselves, I want to grow, I want to be better, and I am willing to do what it takes to get there. This mind-set will get you to the next level, and will enable you to achieve greater and better things.

Visualize the benefits of increased abilities:

Keep your values in the forefront of your mind. This will saturate your mind with the motivation that is required to increase your ability to make your dreams come to light.

Understand your weaknesses:

Take some time to consider what areas you are weakest in and focus on them for a while. In your life, the results of this will be more pronounced than the results of getting a little better at something you have already mastered would be.

Attempt greater levels of what you really want to be good at: Stretch yourself in an area that will allow you to see a different perspective on life. And when you see that view, place yourself in the midst. Allow me to pose a question to you:

What are your dreams and goals? Do you have a plan to implement them?

Think about what you would enjoy doing, either for fun or for a living. Write them all down; then prioritize them. Remember, these are your dreams, so you want to take action. This exercise will allow you to do so.

Life is much too short not to pursue your dreams. Remember, these are the dreams and goals that are born out of your heart and mind. These are the goals that are unique to you. They come from who you were created to be and gifted to become. Your specific goals are what you want to attain, because they are what will bring joy and happiness to your life. Keep in mind that your value and self-worth is worth much more than a life that is simply handed to you on a platter.

Make this promise to yourself:

My mission is to go deep within myself and decide what I want out of life. It is to keep trying to improve who I am and what I want to become. It is to make myself proud of who I am for all of my accomplishments, however great or small. From now on, I will turn all negatives that come my way into positives. I realize that each failure is just another lesson to be learned. I promise that I will take charge of the direction and quality of my life. I alone am responsible for me, my actions, and my inaction. I will not blame others for my failures, nor will I allow others to take credit for my successes. I will work diligently and constantly to improve who I am. I will be courageous and face my fears, knowing that in doing so, my strength will increase. I will realize my dreams, one by one. And I will support others in their dreams, as well. This is my life, and I will live it to the fullest.

Stone 16:

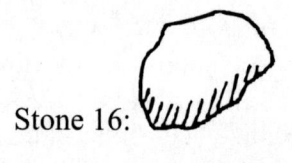

How Do You View Life?
What can I do today that will make a difference?

How do you view life?

How do you view life when things are not going well? You can ask yourself a couple of questions:

What can I do today that will make a difference?
What can I do when all that I have done has not worked?
What can I do when I have run out of time?

We all need a reminder or a boost every now and then. You can do whatever you want to do, despite the most impossible circumstances. Maybe you cannot change the circumstances, but you can change yourself. That is something that you are in charge of.

You are in charge of whether you read, develop new skills, or take new classes. You can change anything you wish to change. If you don't like the way something is going for you, change it. If something does not suit you, change it. If something isn't enough, change it. You can turn all negatives into positives. You can have more than what you have, because you can become more than who you are. That's a big challenge—to become all that you can be.

When you maximize your potential, you stretch your belief in yourself. Change begins with choice. Any day we wish, we can discipline ourselves to make important changes in our lives.

Discipline is the bridge between goals and accomplishments. Lack of discipline is not the fact that you don't do anything. It's what not doing anything will cost you. We all will suffer from one of two pains: the pain of discipline or the pain of regret. The difference is that discipline weighs ounces while regret weighs tons.

Any day we wish, we can start the process of life change. We can also do nothing. We can pretend rather than perform, and we can have doubt rather than confidence. The choice is yours to make.

You have the ability and the responsibility to make better choices beginning today. Ask yourself this question: "Is my life a mission or an intermission?" You cannot allow your repeated errors in judgments to lead you down the wrong path. You must make the choices that will bring new meaning, happiness, and joy to your life. Let me be so bold as to offer this advice for someone seeking and needing to make changes in their life.

If you don't like the way things are, change them. You are not a tree. A tree is just a tree that was planted or that grew by the side of the road. It does not move or change. It grows old right there. If you are not satisfied, don't be like the tree.

You have the ability to say to yourself, "I am bigger and better than any thing that comes up against me. I will fight until I succeed in whatever I have planned—for me, and me alone."

Have so much confidence in yourself that you can go after Moby Dick in a rowboat and take the tartar sauce with you. Our destiny is shaped by our thoughts and actions. We are accountable for our actions, as well as our reactions.

Whatever comes up in your life, ask yourself: Did I cause this obstacle by my own actions or lack of action or did someone else cause them? Sometimes, we just need to view life through a new set of lenses.

New lenses will allow you to revitalize, recharge, and refresh. Then you can begin to prioritize your desires, because I am convinced that "there are none so blind as those that will not see."

Ray Charles is dead now. He could not see, but sometimes, even with a good set of eyes, someone will not see. Evaluation of the past is the first step toward a vision of the future.

At the end of each day, you should play back the tapes of your performances. The results should make you applaud, prod, or chastise yourself. Ask yourself: What have I mastered today? Most of the critical things in life are the little things.

Let's talk about setting goals for yourself.

Goals. There is no telling what you can do when you set goals, believe in them, and most important, act upon them. These goals are for you and you alone.

Sometimes, you need long-range goals to help you past the obstacles. Setting goals will help to make you the person you must be to achieve them. Remember, whatever good thing we build in life will build our character, as well.

I talked with a young man and he told me he was going to barber school. I said to him: "Be the best barber you can be. You might be my barber one day."

I also spoke to a couple of others. One said he wanted to be a business owner and the other said he wanted to study a trade. At the end of the conversation, they could see the door opening.

What I want to leave with you is this: It's not too late to do whatever you want to do. If the door is closed, can you see it opening? Success is waiting for you!

Stone 17:

Positive Attitude
What is your positive attitude?

Positive Attitude

When I hear someone say, "Life is hard," I am always tempted to ask, "Compared to what?" All the technology in the world will never replace a positive attitude. Our attitude reveals a lot about us. That's why you should always allow the person inside of you to be who you are on the outside. This will allow you to set new goals, and self-doubt will be replaced by self-awareness.

Sometimes, you have to think about the company you keep, because negativity will bring your self-esteem down to the lowest point. Negativity is a joy-stealer, and while you are working on our self-confidence, you need your self-esteem level to be at a ten.

You know:

Great minds talk about ideas.
Average minds talk about events.
Small minds talk about other people

This is the question: What type of people are you hanging out with? That's a big question to ask when things are not going the way that you wish and it seems like everything is going downhill.

Just believe and act as if it is impossible to fail. Often, the only thing that stands between you and what you want from life is the will to try and the faith to believe that what you wish for is possible. You cannot always look toward tomorrow through yesterday's vision.

We all know our past and understand the present.
Now we can move toward the future.

I met a young man who wants to own his business. He recognizes his past, and now he is looking toward the future with a new perspective. Actually, I met him coming from the G.E.D. program. He realized that his old attitude in life has not taken him and will not get him where he wants to be. He made up his mind that he will not view life from the sidelines anymore. If your old ideals have not taken you where you want to be, then throw them out of your mind's closet.

A closet has the ability to hold and store old, moldy items that are no longer useful. You cannot continue to view life from the sidelines. You have to take charge of your life from now on. You can turn negatives into positives. Then, you can look toward the future with a new perspective in mind, and you will be free to apply what you know in order to get all that you want out of life.

You have time. There is still tomorrow, next week, next month, even next year. But, unless you develop a sense of urgency, the windows of time will be sadly wasted.

So today, as you think anew about your future, begin to take those very important steps in order to make your dreams come to life. What really counts is that all of your dreams should come true and that you have the courage to pursue them.

By keeping your eyes on your goals, you will

- Be able to resolve in advance to develop and cultivate an attitude of calm, confidence, and positive expectations for yourself.
- Take complete control of your thinking and concentrate on the solution, rather than the problem.

- Look for the good in every situation.
- Be positive and cheerful, no matter what.

The young man who wants to become a business owner now has a renewed mind and a new outlook on life. He can begin to bridge the gap between where he is now and where he wants to be. Remember, obstacles are what you see when you take your eyes off your goals. So you have to resolve in advance to persist until you succeed, no matter what the difficulty may be. Everything of value requires attention and discipline. Even our thoughts require disciple. We must consistently determine our inner boundaries and our code of conduct; otherwise, our though patterns will become confused, and confused thoughts produce confused results.

Just remember: Don't ever say, "If I could, I would." Instead, say, "If I can, I will." Now that you have learned to free your mind from "I can't", now start thinking, "I can."

Now, you will feel good about taking risks. You will be daring, now that your mind has been transformed. And when those complete transformations occur, you will have a different view of everyday life and of the visions for yourself. Because now you can:

- Dare to go forward
- Follow through on your visions
- Refuse to compromise
- Stick to your plans
- Stand for what you believe in
- Avoid the comfort zone (sometimes it can hinder our plans)
- Set huge goals for yourself, even when there is no guarantee of attaining them in sight.

In closing, why not be as a tree? It would be a worthy challenge for us all to stretch upward and outward to the full measure of our capabilities.

Why not do all that we can, every moment that we can, the best that we can, for as long as we can?

Now you can start your "I can" list and discard the "I can't" list.

Stone 18: Finding the Right Path in Life

Finding the Right Path in Life

The importance of finding a career that you will be happy with cannot be overstated. There are many people today whose career does not make them happy. We do not have to conform any more. We can be totally transformed by renewing our mind. Once our mind is renewed, we can find the path that is right for us.

When will this transformation begin? Well, you need a personal mission statement. This can be "My past is my motivation for my future."

It starts the moment you decide to change. That's why it's vital for you to stop for a moment and come face to face with one aspect of your life that needs immediate action. It is truly amazing to see young minds at work, but it is very disheartening to see a mind go to waste and eventually give up because of a lack of hard work and commitment.

That is why you should search deep within your heart in order to find the right path for you. And while you are searching:

Don't wish it were easier—wish you were better.
Don't wish for fewer problems—wish for more skills.
Don't wish for fewer challenges—wish for more wisdom.

Tell yourself, I am empowered from within. I have everything I need to go forth and find whatever it is that I want out of life.

When you make a decision that will affect your life, you need to keep three people in mind: me, myself, and I. Because whatever decision you make will affect you first.

When we are passionate about something, we have to look deep into our heart and soul and fulfill our dreams.
Your dreams and passions do not dissipate or dissolve with time. That's why we need to go inside and execute whatever we are passionate about.

For years, I wanted to work with young people. Now that I am retired, I am fulfilling my dreams. I was blessed with a good job, good benefits—the whole works. But that is not what I wanted to do. So I am pleading with you all: Do not wait until you get my age to do what you want to do. The desire will not go away.

Remind yourself that the future belongs to you, so you have to be relentless in your efforts. It usually does not happen overnight, but it can and will happen. Each of us has a talent of some type inside of us, but we also have two distinct choices to make:

First Choice:

We can be less than what we can be, earn less, have less, read less, and think less. Making these choices will lead to a life of unfulfillment.

Second Choice:

We can do it all, become all we can possibly be, read more, earn more, share life with others, and strive to produce and accomplish as much as we possibly can.

It all boils down to this: You can be or not be whomever or whatever you want to be. Always allow who you are on the inside to be who you are on the outside. Just remember, the worth of your life comes not from what you do or who you know, but from who you are. You are very important.

Education should be high on your list of priorities. It is one of the keys to becoming successful and happy. Once you are on the path to believing in yourself, you will be able to expand your territory and be more innovative and creative in your decision-making.

Remember, the choices you make will be for yourself, and your choices do have consequences, sometimes good and sometimes bad. The choices you make will affect you, so ask yourself: Will this be good or bad for me?

Finding the right path in life is so important that it takes all our efforts to decide what it is that will make us truly happy. Keep in mind that if your life is built on a solid foundation of values, honesty, and self-worth, you will have a better chance of reaching your goals.

Doing this, you will cultivate an unshakable character within yourself. When the winds of life cause changes to come about, we must change. We must struggle to our feet once more and keep looking toward our destination with a positive outlook.

Nothing good has ever been achieved except by those who dared to believe that something inside them was superior to any circumstance. We generally change ourselves for one of two reasons: inspiration or desperation. If we look at desperation in a positive way, it will make us more determined to make some changes.

We should adopt the ant philosophy. The ant never quits. If an ant is headed someplace and you try to stop it, it will look for another way to go where it wants to go. It will climb over, under, and around. An ant never quits trying to go where it wants to go.

The only thing that stands between a person and what he or she wants from life is the will to try and the faith to believe that it is possible. Just believe and act as if it is impossible to fail. You are creating your future life with your present thinking, because the future is purchased by the present. Convince yourself that you can succeed, and you will.

Every living creature that comes into the world has something allotted to him to perform. Therefore, one should not just stand by and be a spectator. For a person to achieve all that is demanded of him or her, he must regard himself as greater than he is.

The recipe for success is this:
Study while others are sleeping,
Work while others are not,
Prepare while others are playing,
And dream while others are wishing.

You know days are expensive. When you spend a day, you have one less day to spend. So make sure you spend each day wisely.

Remember, you cannot allow anything or any circumstance to abort your future opportunities.

Stone 19:

Diversity
I have the freedom to choose

Diversity

According to Webster, diversity means that which is diverse or which varies. We live in a society where we have choices. The fact that we all have a destiny makes it easier to work toward our goals and visions.

Now, we can work on our integrity and excellence, or just be mediocre. We have that choice.

If something or someone has impacted your life and you have been profoundly touched or strongly felt the results, you must take this to the next level. You must pursue your own directions. Diversity will allow you to go in many different directions.

Opportunity plus ability equals accountability. In the diverse society that we live in, there are so many opportunities, and if we have ability, we are accountable to ourselves first. We can develop our own self-worth as it pertains to our own lives and careers, because being satisfied has a lot to do with our attitude. Whether we choose to make a career move or we offer ourselves to help another person or organization, we have an opportunity to give something back.

And since there is so much diversity in our society, we don't have to borrow anyone else's plan for our lives. We can develop our own plans, and then we can come up with ways to satisfy our soul, heart, and mind. This will indeed allow us to expand our territory. To expand your mind, step outside of your comfort zone.

When this happens, we will become aware of the fact that we are empowered from the inside to go forth in any direction that appeals to us.

One thing we have to keep in mind is that success is a path following which you can easily lose your way. Sometimes, we can forget that we need a lantern of reality and a compass of flexibility. At times, we do have to be flexible. Because of the fact that we do have a vast array of choices, we don't have to conform to anything we don't like or anything we are not satisfied with, because our outer world should be a reflection of our inner world.

We can be relentless in our efforts, because the society we live in is so diverse. For example, I grew up in a large family of ten, and we are all different. We all made different career choices, but we all come together, have a common bond and agree on certain things. Each of us has a destiny or a purpose in life. Each of us could go in a different direction and find his or her purpose. As humans, we share much, yet no one questions the diversity of our thought patterns or behavioral styles.

For example, one person just wants to get a job done as soon as possible. Another wants to do the job with other people. Another wants to do the job and not ruffle anyone's feathers. Yet another wants to do the job with integrity. Each will take a different approach to reach the same end.

With diversity, it should not surprise us to see different people react differently to the same situations. We are all innovated and destined to follow our path in life. It is said that variety is the spice of life. But we need to prioritize things in our lives so we can make the right choices, because our choices do have consequences. If our plan is to rise to the next level, we all must do certain things:

- set new goals
- believe in our goals
- have the urgency for action
- seek new challenges
- always decide what's right before deciding what's possible
- never allow our memories to be greater than our dreams

I have huge dreams for myself, and they far outweigh my past memories, because we cannot become who we want to be by remaining who we are.

Stone 20:

Change—the Power of Choice
My own power of choice

Change—the Power of Choice

As the winds change, the flow of the river changes, and the birds change their direction, we can make changes in our lives. Change began to take on a new meaning when I realized one morning I was getting older. Then I decided that I must make some changes in my life—now!

I took a retrospective view of my life and concluded that I have had a very good life. I have eaten whatever I wanted to eat, and as much of it as I wanted.
I drank as much soda, instead of water, as I wanted to drink. I ate as much bread and sweets as I wanted.
I did very little exercise. My path and direction never changed. Then, the word change became illuminated in my mind, and I gave it some serious thought.

Change means to alter or make different, to shift, to quit, and to exchange. With my own choice of omissions, I now have a much greater commission. I thought to exchange my soda for water! It was time to make some changes. On any given day, we can discipline ourselves to make changes in our lives. On any given day, we can start a new activity. On any given day, we can start the process of changing our lives.

We can do it immediately, next week, next month, or next year. We are all empowered with whatever we need to make changes in our lives. I thought my 5-C Step program would be good. The 5-C program is this:

1) Comprehend the importance of making changes.
2) Choose the changes that are right for me.
3) Conquer my sweet tooth or craving.

4) Communicate and share my goals with others for support.
5) Commit to the choices that I've made.

In times of rapid change in our society, we must constantly re-evaluate ourselves, taking into consideration the new realities that surround us. We can transform ourselves any time we wish. Sometimes we have to take risks and be daring for a complete transformation to take place.

Sometimes our circumstances are created by our own choices. We have the ability to change every aspect of our life by starting today, forgetting yesterday, and looking toward tomorrow. Before anything can happen, we need to ask: When was the last time I made a change in my life for me, and me alone?

When was the last time we looked at our surroundings? Do we see anything new, or do we see the same things we've been looking at for a long time? Are they positive or negative?

The closet of our mind holds old ideas, dreams, pain, hurts, disappointments—the list goes on and on. But it also holds new ideas and goals, so we cannot afford to let them become buried under all the moldy and outdated stuff that's been hanging around much too long. Our power of speech is an investment in the change that is about to take place. The tongue has the ability to speak both negative and positive words and ideas.

What are we listening to? Now is the time to get our old ideas behind us and look to the future. It all begins with our very own power of choice. Change is a projection of the mind, but it must be well defined in order to overpower all the obstacles that get in your way. Changes can be positive if we look at the 5-C Step method. Yesterday's passion may not serve tomorrow's goals. We cannot continue to look to the future through yesterday's eyes.

I now drink more water, eat ninety-five percent fewer sweets and breads, and walk and work out at least five or six times a week. I am no longer obsessed with soda. Because of these changes, I now have an attitude of gratitude. Now I see that everything begins and ends with my own power of choice.

Stone 21:

Lessons Learned
If you want something out of life, become relentless in your efforts

Lydia M. Douglas

Lessons Learned

To the old adage, "If life hands you lemons, make lemon-aid," attach the phrase, "Just keep adding a little sweetener along the way." Life will hand out a few lemons, but I realize that if they had been handed to me free, then the value would be less meaningful. One of the secrets to success is to have an ideal mixed with inspiration. My parents taught us, "If you want something out of life, become relentless in your efforts and never give up." After all, results are the best measure of human progress—not conversation, explanation, or justification. Results!

Another thing I've learned is to be passionate about learning. Then I can share information with a great deal of inspiration. I have also learned that direction determines the destination. So I asked myself is this the direction I want to take in my life? Is this someone else's direction? Is it my parents' direction, my spouse's, or my children's? Or is it mine? I can allow others to educate and inform me, but I have to let the decisions be a product of my own conclusions.

I have learned that, once you get to a certain level in your life or profession, you must not just get comfortable, but keep looking upward to the next level. Achieving your vision does not mean you've reached the end of the line. It simply means you've come to a new starting point. Discipline is the bridge between goals and accomplishments. It isn't the fact that you haven't accomplished your goals; it's what it will cost you if you don't.

My father also taught me to do more than you get paid for, because it will be an investment in your future. I did not understand this when he said it. Now, I know that the miracle of the seed and the soil is not available through affirmation. It is only available through labor. I have leaned that I should take the ant philosophy. The ant works all summer long. He works all the time, looking toward the next day or the next winter.

With that in mind, I now expect the best, plan for the worst, and prepare to be surprised. And with all of that, I now know what I have to do to take control of my life. My parents taught us what was right and wrong, but it is up to me to stay within the boundaries of principals and morals. I try to decide what's right before I decide what's possible. At the end of each day, the results of my performance will applaud, prod, or chastise me.

We will all have a harvest time in our lives, when we will be able to look back and see what we have produced, either through our own lives, our children's lives, or even our grandchildren's lives. What have we accomplished? What can we share with others? Have our lives made any impact on anyone?

By sharing the lessons I have learned, a transformation took place in the life of one of my co-workers. If we share our lessons and experiences with others, it should all be about results, not who we know or where we live or where we've been.

Sometimes, it's our life story that is the basis for affecting people. In that case, we will be able to share information with a great deal of inspiration, because we care enough to try and make a difference in another person's life.

After I shared something with one of my co-workers, she and her husband became able to buy a house, and they can pay their daughter's tuition for study at USLM. They have another child getting ready to go in the fall. A successful life is not in what we have, but who we have become. Knowing is not enough, we must apply the knowledge. Willing is not enough, we must do. So, let's make sure that the lessons of our lives become examples and not warnings to stay away or stay clear.

Life is an ongoing process of keeping your visions and values before you and aligning your life to be congruent with or equal to those things that are embedded deep down inside you. The quality of life is far more important than the quantity. These are just some of the lessons I've learned.

Stone 22:
Pain Relievers for Your Mind—800 Milligrams

Lydia M. Douglas

Pain Relievers for Your Mind—800 Milligrams

You must learn to translate wisdom into labor.

I use to say, "I hope things change soon." Then I learned that if I change, things will change.

Don't say, "If I could, I would." Say, "If I can, I will."

You can't make progress without making decisions.

A tree never moves out of its place. Don't be like the tree.

Learn to express, not impress. Know the difference.

Maybe you cannot change your destination, but you can change your direction.

If you don't like the way things are going, change it.

Good communication starts and ends with good preparation.

The best motivation is self-motivation.

Discipline is the bridge between goals and accomplishments.

We must learn to apply all that we know so we can attract all that we want.

The formula for disaster is this: could + should + won't.

Don't set your goals too low. Take them to the next level.

Ideas are information taking shape.

Don't join an easy crowd. You won't grow.

Attitude is greatly shaped by influence and association.

Start a journal. Keep a record of your thoughts.

Stone 23:

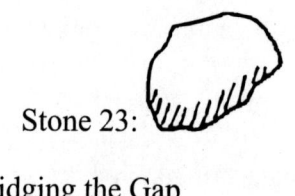

Bridging the Gap

Bridging the Gap

While you are on your quest for a career that will make you happy, allow me to share with you a true testament to how it can happen. A young man who I will call Reggie wanted to work on computers. At the time, the high school he was attending did not have a computer lab. But the school provided transportation for anyone to go to a technical school and study computers. He took advantage of the opportunity and studied during his junior and senior years. When graduated, he joined the marines.

During his twelve years in the military, he did not go to the battlefield at all. He worked in the computer department all of that time. That was the result of his bridging the gap between where he was and where he wanted to be. As time went on, he realized that what he could do on the computer was limited in the military. When he was discharged, he took a job at AT&T, where is still employed today. He is in upper management and is happy and content with his choices.

So, you can bridge the gap between where you are now and where you want to be. All you have to do is figure out what it is that you want to do and go for it.

Stone 24: Defining your Self-worth and Values

Defining your Self-worth and Values

In the eyes of others, how are you perceived? Are you defined by who you are or by what you do? While talking with three young men who were smokers and drinkers, I asked the question: How do you want others to see you? By your container or by the contents of the container, the container being your outer form?

They gave a little though to what I was saying, and their answer was by the contents of themselves. I shared with them the fact that I used to try to smoke and drink, but not anymore. I can laugh, talk, and have as much fun as any one else without it. So I am perceived by the contents of my person, not by the container. We cannot do anything about this outer person, but we are responsible for the inner person.

Now, they no longer want to be identified as "Joe, the smoker" or "Mike, the drinker." We should always allow who we are on the inside to be seen by others on the outside. How do you want to be identified?

Stone 25:

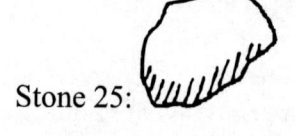

Fulfilling your Dreams

Fulfilling your Dreams

I will give just one example of how you can start the process of fulfilling your dreams. First, start by knowing what it is that you want to attain in life, and become adamant about it. I was in a fast food restaurant. The waitress was a very nice young lady. I asked her if she was in school. Her reply was, "I am waiting on my G.E.D scores to come back." She said she had missed so many days of school due cancer that she did not graduate. She said she was going to the University of Missouri in St. Louis (UMSL). Her desire was to study and do research in medicine. She wanted to help find a cure for cancer.

This came from her heart of hearts. It touched my heart, as well. This young lady is well on her way to fulfilling her dreams.

Stone 26:
Success

Success

What is success? According to Webster, it is a favorable accomplishment. In order to be successful in life, you must have a sense of purpose. First, figure out what your purpose is. We are all created and destined to achieve something in life. We all must find our "something." When you make up your mind what goals you want to achieve in life, it will come to pass.

If you are on your path to success, the way might become dim sometimes. Remember that you will need a lantern of reality and a compass of flexibility at the times when you have to be flexible.

We don't always know immediately what our purpose is. We might have to try two or three things or travel down a different avenue in order to find it. If we search, we will find it.

Ask yourself these questions:

1. What is my purpose?
2. What is my destination?
3. What do I need to do in order to get there?
4. How long will it take me to get there?
5. Will this enable me to be financially stable?
6. Will this allow me to be independent or will I be dependent on others?

Are you prepared for detours or roadblocks? There is no free ride in life. Your mind has to be made up for you to be the successful person you want to be.

Every destination requires preparation. First, you need a made-up mind, a willing heart, and a strong spirit. You have to be willing, ready, and able to make changes in your life if necessary. You might have to leave your comfort zone in order to fulfill your dreams.

This will allow you to create the atmosphere for your visions to take root and grow. You will be able to allow new ideas and revelations to come, as well as opportunities. You will then have the courage to pursue whatever comes your way.

When you have a purpose and a mission in life, you must have directions, because your direction determines your destination. Direction helps you to stay focused and to prioritize things in your life. In order to be successful, sometimes you have to say "no" to certain things so that you can say "yes" to your destiny. Your success should never be any less than your best.

When you are on your journey to success and trials come, remember that they come to make you strong. You should only look back to see where you went wrong and what path you took so that you can choose another direction.

When we learn from our past trials, mistakes, and errors, we know we cannot allow ourselves to dwell on them. We must put them in perspective and forge ahead. Past experiences form a large picture that you can drink from. While drinking, you can learn what's right and what's wrong, what will work for you and what will not. When you look back, both sides will be revealed. Life experiences help shape you into the person you want to become so that you can reach your goals.

In order to be successful you must view life through a new set of lenses. You should always want your future to be better than your past. Make every day count. When you spend one day, it's gone forever; you cannot retrieve it. Even if you only accomplish one thing, it will put you one step closer to your goals. Your journey begins right where you are now, with a made-up mind. This is the first step on your journey. The journey of a thousand miles begins with one step. The Empire State Building began with a single thought in the mind of one person.

Always remember that the ultimate victory in a competition is derived from the inner satisfaction that you gain when you know you have done your best; that you gave all you had from your heart. What leaves the heart of a person will find the hearts of others. Whatever you are striving to do in life will impact others in some way or the other. You can make something happen now. Write down your goals and plans. Then, begin to prioritize them, one plan at a time. If something needs to be eliminated, eliminate it.

Success is the result of your actions and faithfulness. There is room at the top for you, no matter what your visions may be. Many opportunities are waiting. If you measure the time it will take you to get your education against a lifetime that is minimal when you are looking at a lifetime of being successful. The good thing it is that no one can take it away from you. Someone can take your possessions, but no one can take the knowledge you have acquired.

Look up and take your mark. Your ventures are about to begin. Why not be the one to close the gap between image and reality?

Stone 27:

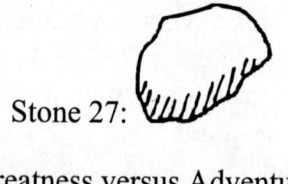

Greatness versus Adventure

Greatness versus Adventure

Greatness—admirable, uncommonly gifted, mighty!

When you step into greatness, your mind set will change. It will say, "My future will be better than my past." As you make the right choices in life and become persistent and patient, you will watch yourself cross the finishing line of your career. We all have a level of greatness within us—we just need to bring it into focus.

Looking toward greatness will raise your self-esteem. This will give rise to a more determined and dedicated mission of fulfilling your dreams.

After all, your choices have consequences—and your choices will affect you first. You are on your own path. When you make decisions, think about three people: me, myself, and I. No matter what level of greatness you are on, if you are clear, the world will respond with clarity.

On the way to greatness, set your sights straights ahead and focus in on your vision. Do not hang around substandard people. If your company cannot help fuel your dreams, maybe that's your cue. After all, you are influenced by your associations. If you hang around thinkers, you will be a better thinker; around planners, you will be a better planner. It goes on and on, encompassing every aspect of your life. You have managed to get where you are now. Don't waste time with idle chat that will get you nowhere. You are smart, brilliant, and unique, and you have great potential and possibilities.

You have a purpose in life. Focus on finding and fulfilling that purpose, which may be one or many. The key is to find it and unlock its doors. You cannot allow yourself to fall under the influence of others. When you view life through your own lenses, you can and will see yourself doing whatever you want to do and becoming the person you want to become.

Now that you have reached this point, you are no longer confused about what direction to go in. You are well on your way to finding the path that's right for you. Adventure, according to Webster, is a bold undertaking, taking chances, and venturing to dare.

Adventures will come and cloud your mind at times. Do not allow anything or anyone to turn you aside. You are either going somewhere in your life, or you are going nowhere. Somewhere is always better than nowhere. The adventures of life come in the form of going to the mall, watching movies, and skate boarding with friends, or just hanging out doing nothing. The adventures of life will not allow you to face new challenges, seize new opportunities, test your resources against the unknown, and discover your own unique potentials.

We all have our strengths and weaknesses. When we recognize the fact that they are part of our life, we will be able to focus on our strengths, rather than our weaknesses. You have a choice. You can look at adventure in a negative manner or a positive one. When it comes, if it does not motivate and inspire you, turn away from it. It will so easily throw you off track, away from your goals.

When you look at or think about famous people, say to yourself, "If they can do it, so can I."

On your way to greatness, you will find many ways to do things, but you should always figure out what's right before you make your decision. When you are determined and ambitious, you need to follow the right path in order to reach your destination.

Having a clear idea of where you are heading will eliminate or reduce time loss. Once time is lost, it cannot be regained. Sometimes detours may occur, but don't get derailed. Stay on track.

Remember, this is your journey. Having a clear idea will help you know who you are and what you want to become. We each have an enormous reservoir of resources within us, just waiting to be revealed. Every action you take will move you one step closer to your goal. Greatness versus adventure! You are creating your tomorrow through your actions today.

Stone 28:
This Is My Season

This Is My Season

We all go through seasons. We have no control over this, but we do have control over how we react to the changes that come into ours lives. While we are in the middle of this change or season, we are accountable for our actions. Now that the winter of your life has passed, pull off the extra clothes or baggage that you were wearing, and allow your body and mind to breathe.

Now that you have made it through this season, it's time for a new attitude toward your life. Spring is quite different than winter. Winter is harsh, and spring is a time for a new beginning. There is new grass, fresh flowers, new leaves on the trees, and a new you! Allow your mind to breathe new thoughts and dream new dreams. Set different goals for yourself.

Winter was cold. Now it's time to look in another direction. Opportunities are there. It's up to you to move toward them. We plan for a new harvest in the springtime.
In order to reap you must sow. You have control over how much you reap. If you only sow a little for your future, a little is all you are going to reap. It's harvest time! Do not allow the harvest to pass as a void. It's time to make some choices and decisions for your life. Even though there may be rocks and stony ground on your path, plant anyway. If you plant many seeds, some will take root and grow.

Don't just look in one direction—look in many. Then decide which one is right for you. It is okay to change your mind, as long as you pick and choose a new direction.
We live in a very diverse society, and diversity will allow you to go in many directions. Now, it's time to get to work. First thing first! Remove all of the weeds from your life

and all the negative communication that surrounds you. Eventually, you will uncover your spirit. To do this, you may have to change your location, your friends, or your foes.

If people cannot help to fertilize your dreams, you must give a second thought to offering your time to them. Tune out the shallow voices, and you will have more time to tune in to valuable ones. Seasons are short-lived; it's up to you to make your mark. Your dreams and desires are all inside you, but it is up to you to take them to the next level. It might not happen overnight, but it will never happen if you don't give it a try.

Take a moment to envision yourself in the position you want to be in. If you want to be an attorney, place yourself in the courtroom. If you want to be a nurse, place yourself at the nurses station in the hospital. Just tell yourself: "If they can do it, so can I." A rule to follow that worked for me is "If you want something out of life, be relentless in your efforts to get it, and never give up."

A beautiful garden will be the result of your harvest. After all, results are the best measure of human progress, not conversation, explanation, or justification. Results will speak for themselves. If you do not try, you will not succeed. Opportunity will not come and knock on your door—you must do the knocking. There are many doors out there; do not allow them to remain closed in your life.

In life, you can achieve whatever results you truly desire through hard work, dedication, and a level of desire that no one can take away from you. It's up to you. No one else can fill your shoes. Whatever you were chosen to do in life is set aside for no one but you. Do all you can during this season, and when it has passed, you will look back and say, "Well done!"

You are standing on the shoulders of some great leaders, who have proven that whatever you want can come to pass through hard work and persistence. Through this, you will be able to reap the harvest that you have labored for. Your success in life depends on the choices you make. Your choices have consequences, sometimes good and sometimes bad. If you have worked hard to bring your dreams to life, you can sit back and smell the roses of your harvest. Opportunity plus ability equals accountability.

Stone 29:
Mission Statement

Mission Statement

What is your mission statement? A mission statement is when you define yourself, your purpose, your values, your goals, and your intentions. What will others gain from you through what you have to offer?

A mission gives you a sense of direction, a purpose. We should not be doing or saying anything just because we can. Our values and self-worth are defined by our actions and speech. Just because our mouth can speak, we should not allow it to say anything. Our heart listens to what our mouth is saying. What leaves the mouth reaches the heart.

Now back to my question: What is your mission statement?
- Is it to learn more?
- Is it to read more?
- Is it to reach out more?
- Is it to be better today than you were yesterday?
- What are you passionate about?
- What lurks deep within your heart?

On your mission, you must have a great deal of passion for what you are going to do. Passion will allow you to take control of your life and to become more capable of setting the standards for your life.

There is a big difference between a job and a career. A job is something you do because you need the money. It often comes with regret and frustration. A career is something you do because you enjoy it and it brings a great deal of joy into your life. When you enjoy your career, you will give it your best; you will put your heart into it.

You will always do well in what you love. Your life begins and ends with you being happy and content. Starting right now, chase those dreams with everything you have, and you will have no regrets. You must be committed to your mission. Your personal integrity is on the line. Others will measure you, your success, and your dedication by it.

Don't tarnish your goals by giving up because the task got hard. Erase "give up" from your vocabulary. What if Henry Ford had given up? We would not have the Ford cars and trucks that we have today. Only persistence, faith, courage, and hard work enable you to learn about the person with whom you share your mirror. Always keep your integrity, your values, and your self-worth in the forefront. Without them, your goal becomes no more than a vision. Lacking them is like having a slow leak in a tire: it will slowly but eventually render the tire worthless. Remember, this is your mission statement regarding promises you are making to yourself.

What's at stake is profoundly more important than the goal itself. In the balance hangs the essence of your life. It causes you to measure your character and overall success. Without a positive mission in your life, you will find yourself going in many directions without focus. Without focus, you are on a dead end road with a crash sight ahead.

You will now be encouraged to keep your dreams alive and to cross the finishing line of your career. Personal integrity and values are the essential assets that will move you closer to your goals and to success. Keep everything breathing with the oxygen of integrity. Preparing your mission statement involves overhauling yourself so that you may see all the flaws and install new ideas. When others see your commitment to yourself, they will embrace your dreams, too. Whatever career you choose, give it your all. Take a minute to organize and prioritize.

There is nothing more important than your belief in yourself. Every day, you will see yourself camouflaged in the value you have for yourself. Be sure to build quality into your mission statement. Doing this will allow you to expand your territory. There are no limitations to what or whom you can become other than the ones you place on yourself. Always believe in yourself. If you don't, no one else will.

Remind yourself when you look in the mirror, that you are writing your tomorrow based on what you do and accomplish today. Today is yesterday's tomorrow. You can chart your own future only when you know the path that led you to where you are now. Whatever career you choose, make sure you have the inner spirit for it. For example, does it involve children? Do you have patience with children? Does it involve older people? Do you have patience with older adults? Always chose the right path for you. After all, you are expected to give of yourself to others. What's the point of setting a mission if, when you succeed, you realize it's not right for you? That would be a waste of time.

What are the rewards for your choices? Will they be financial? Will you have self-satisfaction? It doesn't matter who you are or how much you make. It's who or what you have become. You have the key to become successful. It's your birthright. We are all destined to become something in life so that we can give back to others. What we have is a loan. When we share what we have with others, we shall know we are on the right track. Be still and know the work that is about to take place inside you.

Your mind is not feeding on negativity anymore. It's rejoicing in all the positive images that run through it. A mind is a terrible thing to waste. Now you will be able to create the unshakeable character that you have the potential to be.

While you are preparing your mission statement, think about the saying in the computer environment, "GI-GO", garbage in, garbage out. Whatever you put into your own life is what you will get back.

Plan as far into your future as you can. You can and will reap the benefits of your hard work and labor. The quality, not the longevity, of one's life is what is important. —Dr. Martin Luther King, Jr.

Shalom. Peace.

Stepping Stones

"I do not ask to walk smooth paths nor to bear an easy load. I pray for strength and fortitude to climb the rock-strewn road. Give me such courage so that I can scale the hardest peaks alone and transform every stumbling block into a stepping stone."

—Gale Brook Burket

Reviews

"The wisdom expressed by Mrs. Douglas in her book I believe will be embraced by parents and students alike. A work that is well done!" Linda Harris, Classroom teacher

"Mrs. Douglas has incorporated a variety of approaches in her book to address the need for building self-confidence in middle and high school students."
Ruby Ellis, 4th grade teacher

"Lydia's writing is very insightful for all ages, but she clearly wants to help the youths."
Charlotte Petty, Editor and Publisher of The Spanish Lake Word

"I read an excerpt entitled "Focus" and afterwards I felt encouraged and motivated to continue striving towards my goals." Jasmane G. Boyd, Student, University City High School

"I was impressed with Mrs. Douglas from the moment I met her. She is very inspirational and will touch many lives with her words." Victoria Whitfield, Founder of Victorian House for Pregnant Homeless Teens